W9-CQT-770

A Peaceable Season

This portrait of Edward Hicks was painted by Thomas Hicks, his first cousin and student, in 1838 when Thomas was sixteen.

EDWARD HICKS

A Peaceable Season

INTRODUCTION BY ELEANORE PRICE MATHER

THE PYNE PRESS
Princeton

Acknowledgments. The Publishers wish to thank the individual and institutional owners of the paintings reproduced here for their courteous cooperation. They gratefully acknowledge the assistance so freely offered them by Miss Alice Ford and Miss Jane Rittenhouse of the Friends Historical Library at Swarthmore College.

Sources. Most of the passages in these pages were published originally in *Memoirs of the Life and Religious Labors of Edward Hicks, Late of Newtown, Bucks County, Pennsylvania. Written by Himself*, Philadelphia: Merrihew & Thompson, 1851. The pages on which they appear in the *Memoirs* are as follows: *A kingdom that is not of this world*, 56; *Such then was George Washington*, 357; *Our Saviour has promised*, 349; *And I soon got into a state*, 51–52; *Today I think I have been edified*, 147–148; *Industriously engaged at my trade*, 149; *David Twining was, . . . It was this woman*, 21, 24; *I quit the only business*, 71; *Finally, my friends, farewell*, 330–331. The passage beginning *I am induced to believe* is from a Sermon Hicks delivered at Green Street Meeting, Philadelphia, August 19, 1827; the passages *For if the Lord preserve us* and *Where, then can a man* are from a Sermon delivered at Carpenters' Hall, Philadelphia, on the same date. Both were published in *The Quaker*, II, No. 4, Philadelphia, 1827, pages 145–207; 172, 203, 202. The poem on the last page was published in Alice Ford's *Edward Hicks: Painter of the Peaceable Kingdom*, Philadelphia, University of Pennsylvania Press, 1952 (page 41), the standard volume on Hicks's work and life.

On the cover. Peaceable Kingdom (1844). This painting was delivered to Joseph Watson in the autumn of 1844, with a note from Hicks characterizing it as "one of the best paintings I ever done." Courtesy of Abby Aldrich Rockefeller Folk Art Collection.

Library of Congress Catalog Number 73-79523

SBN 87861-052-9

Printed by Pearl Pressman-Liberty, Philadelphia

Manufactured in the United States of America

Distributed by Charles Scribner's Sons, New York

Introduction

Although I had scarcely reached my eighteenth year, the sound of war being heard in our land, I enrolled myself as a soldier, delighted with the martial music and the feathered foppery of the regimentaled dandy.

MEMOIRS OF THE LIFE AND RELIGIOUS
LABORS OF EDWARD HICKS

Who would believe that within a few years this feathered fop would don the drab coat of a Quaker preacher, or that, in the cultural history of America, his name would become identified with peace? Certainly no one would have credited it who knew him in his adolescence. For Edward Hicks was then a coachmaker's apprentice, reveling in fast company, lewd talk, and long draughts of the hard liquor with which the completion of each carriage was traditionally celebrated.

But two narrow brushes with death changed the pattern of his life. Despondent and dissatisfied with himself, he went on lonely Sunday walks through the Pennsylvania countryside. One of these rambles through the lanes of his native Bucks County took him to the door of the Middletown Friends Meeting House, and he went in.

The bare whitewashed walls, the plain garments of the worshippers, and, above all, the silence must have brought back to him the Quaker training of his childhood. He had not been born a Friend. His parents, Isaac and Catherine Hicks, belonged to the Church of England, as did his grandfather, Gilbert Hicks, the Tory Chief Justice of Bucks County.

They were people of privilege, which was swept away with the American Revolution. Born in 1780, in the midst of the Revolutionary War, the future artist was left motherless when Catherine Hicks died on the day of the British surrender at Yorktown.

A kindly Quakeress, Elizabeth Twining, had taken Edward into her household, and her teaching, though forgotten in his adolescent years, came back to him later. When, having finished his apprenticeship, he became the junior partner of a coachmaker in Milford (now Hulmeville), he stipulated that he have time off to attend mid-week meeting. He joined the Society of Friends in 1803, and in the same year married his childhood sweetheart, Sarah Worstall.

They settled in Milford and borrowed money to build a house. This was the beginning of the financial troubles which plagued him all his life. The arrival of children, four girls and a boy, did not help matters. Nor did his religious calling.

Friends had no professional ministry at that time. Out of the worshipping silence might come an inner summons to speak, and at the same time a fearful reluctance. Hicks was torn by this conflict, but at length yielded and spoke, afterward feeling tremendous relief. Since his gift was approved by his meeting he felt called to travel in the ministry. This took him throughout Bucks County, to Philadelphia, Wilmington, Baltimore, and New York—and as far afield as Canada. Friends' ministers were not paid, and these journeys placed a heavy burden on his slender finances.

To augment his income he began to paint signs—for streets, shops, and taverns. Tavern signs are the missing link between Hicks the coachmaker and Hicks the artist. They required him to draw figures and, in a limited way, to handle composition. Their medieval flavor lingers in his banners with lettered inscriptions, his *couchant* leopard, his lion with its solar mane.

Apparently, some time after he moved to Newtown, Hicks took up easel painting. The primitive artist found a source of instruction in the engraved reproductions which served as Bible illustrations then. We learn from Alice Ford's excellent biography, *Edward Hicks: Painter of the Peaceable Kingdom* (Philadelphia, 1952), that he borrowed his *Peaceable Kingdom of the Branch* from a British artist, Richard Westall. Based on the prophecy of Isaiah, who foretold the coming of the Messiah, when "the wolf also shall lie down with the lamb," the composition consisted of a trustful child surrounded by friendly beasts.

This became Hicks's favorite theme. In his many painted versions of it—more than fifty are known—he introduced, after the manner of the primitive artist, certain curiously localized features such as the Natural Bridge of Virginia, the Delaware Water Gap, and Penn's Treaty with the Indians, the last of which appears in almost all the *Peaceable Kingdom's*. For the artist/preacher believed that Penn's settlement of Pennsylvania was a practical attempt to realize the Kingdom of God on earth.

These additions reflect the painter's intense Americanism and identification with the young republic. We also find this enthusiasm for the American scene in his *Falls of Niagara,* with its distinctively American animals, moose, beaver, eagle, and rattlesnake, and in his *George Washington at the Delaware*—a dramatic figure on horseback beneath a pale moon and cloud-wracked sky.

But his greatest hero was William Penn. Hicks saw Penn not only as a Quaker peacemaker but also as a defender of liberty. Because Penn had suffered much persecution in England, he had granted unprecedented civil and religious liberties to his colonists in the New World. And Hicks, by the late 1820's, was particularly sensitive to the issue of religious liberty. In his own Society of Friends he felt pressures that threatened freedom of belief. Friends were dividing into two groups: the Orthodox, who placed their emphasis on the Bible and the atonement of Christ, and the Hicksites, who stressed the Holy Spirit, or, as they termed it, the Inner Light.

The latter were followers of Elias Hicks, a cousin to whom the artist was devoted. Edward threw himself into the fray with partisan zeal, defending his cause with complete sincerity, but wounding many persons in the doing. The peaceable kingdom of the Quaker community was cleft in twain. A formal Separation took place in 1827.

As an aftermath of this conflict a new psychological dimension enters the artist/preacher's canvases. The animals are no longer mere beasts; in certain instances they become studies in human character. The meaning of these *Kingdom* animals he expounded in a sermon at Goose Creek Meeting, Loudon County, Virginia, in 1837. All mankind, said the preacher, falls into one of four temperaments: melancholy, sanguine, phlegmatic, or choleric. These temperaments are symbolized respectively by the gloomy and avaricious wolf, the lustful and volatile leopard, the worldly-wise and indifferent bear, and the proud and angry lion. When these are redeemed by the Inner Light they are spiritually reborn into their domestic opposites, the gentle and loving lamb, kid, cow, and ox.

In Hicks's later *Kingdoms* we feel a peculiar identity with the lion and leopard. Indeed, in the character of the artist himself we see something of both—and also something of the bantam rooster of his farmscapes. He was contentious and fiercely prejudiced. (The pugnacity is apparent in the portrait painted by his cousin Thomas Hicks—though the portrait also reveals a man who inwardly craved peace.) Because of his quick temper he frequently tangled with his fellow members at Newtown Meeting, which he had helped to found, and with his other Bucks County neighbors. And he was haunted by their disapproval of his painting. For Friends of this period deplored pictorial art almost as much as music, dancing, fiction, and the theatre.

Yet Quaker austerity had its compensations. Though Friends rejected beauty in the fine arts, they deeply appreciated the beauty of nature. This is reflected in the lovely farmscapes of Hicks's later years. In *The Residence of David Twining 1787,* we see the home of his childhood, with his beloved foster mother reading the Scriptures to him beneath a shady tree. And in the "May morning view" of *The Leedom Farm* we see other figures from his past, haloed by the gentle resurgence of spring. A mood transcending time brings a touch of the *Kingdom* to the farmscapes. These pastoral scenes are peopled only with the redeemed, those animals which have accepted the discipline of the yoke, and in them the green growth of the countryside becomes one with a new-found tranquility in the artist.

The painter's last years had their sorrows, with the dropping off, one by one, of his old friends. Most poignant was the death of his little granddaughter, Phoebe Ann. His cough, which had been troubling him for years, grew worse. And there were times when the Spirit departed from him and left him desolate.

Yet he had moments of assurance. "The silent part of worship was to me a blessed time," he wrote in his *Memoirs.* And he was painting better and better. He must have realized that his improved techniques and handling of space were enabling him to transfer his new vision of reconciliation to the last *Kingdoms.*

He continued painting through the heat of the summer of 1849. On the twenty-third of August he breathed his last, without apparent pain or suffering. Though he foresaw his approaching death, he told a friend who dropped in at his shop that he had never been so happy. For his concern as a minister, that had rested on him nearly forty years, was removed; and it had left him in peace. He had at last entered that Kingdom which he had preached so long.

ELEANORE PRICE MATHER

The Peaceable Kingdom of the Branch

The wolf also shall dwell with the lamb, and the leopard shall lie down with the kid; and the calf and the young lion and the fatling together; and a little child shall lead them.

And the cow and the bear shall feed; their young ones shall lie down together; and the lion shall eat straw like the ox.

And the sucking child shall play on the hole of the asp, and the weaned child shall put his hand on the cockatrice's den.

They shall not hurt nor destroy in all my holy mountain; for the earth shall be full of the knowledge of the Lord, as the waters cover the sea.

ISAIAH XI: 6–9

THE PEACEABLE KINGDOM OF THE BRANCH
(1825–30)

Hicks found his favorite theme in a drawing by Richard Westall, R.A.
Child and animals derive from the Old Testament prophecy which
foretold the coming of a Messiah, descended from the House of David,
who would restore Israel and bring peace on earth. The "Branch" here
is a symbol for the Messiah. Isaiah's prophecy begins: "And there shall
come forth a rod out of the stem of Jesse [father of David], and a
Branch shall grow out of his roots." Westall identified the Messiah
with Christ by making the Branch a grapevine, symbol of the Eucharist.
Hicks added the Penn's Treaty grouping and the Natural Bridge of
Virginia to the main theme.

The peaceable KINGDOM of the branch.

the lamb,& the leopard shall lie down with the

The wolf also shall dwell with

kid;& the young lion& the fatling

together;& a little child shall lead them.

Falls of Niagara

I am induced to believe that there never was since the creation of the world, such a race of intelligent beings as are now upon the stage of action. I am not one of those who have been induced to believe that the world is growing worse—far from it. I am encouraged, at times, and animated with a hope of better things. The great work of redemption is on the wing, mankind are on the advance, and have been ever since the manifestation of Jesus Christ in the flesh. Whatever may have been the ups and downs on different parts of this globe, and in different periods of the human family, there has been, on the whole, an evident advancement. And in this happy land of America, the advancement has been peculiarly striking. To the intelligent man, who can look back sixty years, what changes and improvements present themselves on every side, and particularly in this city—what changes in the state and country around—what changes in human society—what advancements! What are we not blessed with in this land, that flows, as it were, with milk and honey?

GREEN STREET MEETING

FALLS OF NIAGARA (1825)

In 1819 Hicks visited Niagara Falls on a preaching journey; one can assume that the three small figures represent the painter and his two traveling companions. Alice Ford, Hicks's biographer, finds a further source for the subject in an engraving after a painting by John Vanderlyn. To it the Quaker artist added a decorative border inscribed with verses from "The Foresters," a poem by the American ornithologist, Alexander Wilson. Note the typically New World animals—moose, eagle, beaver, and rattlesnake—in which the intense Americanism of the artist is expressed with pride.

The Falls

Above, below, where'er the astonished eye
Turns to behold, new opening wonders lie,

With uproar hideous first the *Falls* appear,
The stunning tumult thundering on the ear.

This great o'erwhelming work of awful Time
In all its dread magnificence sublime,

Rises on our view, amid a crashing roar
That bids us kneel, and Time's great God adore.

18

Peaceable Kingdom

A kingdom that is not of this world—a kingdom whose subjects never did nor never can fight with carnal weapons; a kingdom that is set up in every immortal soul where *Christ* the Saviour is permitted to enter as a quickening spirit, and rule and reign triumphant; a kingdom where *Christ's* new commandment is received, and true brotherly kindness leads all to love one another as *Christ* loved them. . . . This is the kingdom our blessed *Saviour* established when he said, "My kingdom is not of this world, but now is my kingdom not from hence."

MEMOIRS

PEACEABLE KINGDOM WITH LETTERED BORDER
(ca. 1840)

The artist has transferred a lettered border to a *Peaceable Kingdom,* the prophetic verse inscribed in couplets of his own making. In each corner block is a lamb, symbol of Christ; above it is a dove bearing an olive branch of peace. Written inscriptions, either in borders or on banners, were a primitive touch, lingering from the late Middle Ages. The artist/preacher probably acquired the technique from his experience with sign painting. Hicks went on producing this engaging and decorative sort of *Kingdom* long after he had evolved other categories. This one is a late version of its type. In the background is the Delaware River, which flowed not far from the artist's home in Newtown, Pennsylvania.

The leopard with the harmless kid laid down,
And not one savage beast was seen to frown,

The wolf did with the lambkin dwell in peace,
His grim carnivrous nature there did cease;

The lion with the fatling on did move,
A little child was leading them in love,

When the great PENN his famous treaty made
With indian chiefs beneath the elm tree's shade.

Washington At the Delaware

Such then was George Washington, that distinguished instrument in the hand of the infinitely wise Jehovah, for establishing the American Republic, a system of government the most healthy and happy, the most successful and generous, now under heaven, whose benevolent institutions are becoming more and more the admiration of the world; and while virtue, liberty and independence continue to be esteemed among the children of men, the name of Washington will be pronounced with veneration and respect by millions of intelligent beings.

MEMOIRS

WASHINGTON AT THE DELAWARE (ca. 1834)

With this canvas, Hicks, the sign painter, has become a master of his craft. The sign marked the Jersey side of a covered bridge spanning the Delaware at Washington Crossing. The American Commander-in-Chief came to Newtown the day after his victory at Trenton in December of 1776, and in the artist's time the memory of this heroic exploit was still fresh. Martial and dramatic, the composition was derived from an 1819 painting by Thomas Sully. Nearly identical is a copy made for the Pennsylvania end of the bridge; that sign is now in the Mercer Museum of the Bucks County Historical Society.

Courtesy, Mr. and Mrs. Bertram K. Little. Richard Merrill, photographer.

Penn's Treaty with the Indians

Our Saviour has promised, and will fulfill his promise, that "Where two or three are gathered together in his *name*, there will *he* be in the midst of them." Oh the blessedness of true heavenly devotion! . . . Under the influence of this blessed spirit, my soul feels a sweet union and communion with all God's children in their devotional exercise, whether it is performed in a Protestant meeting house, a Roman cathedral, a Jewish synagogue, an Hindoo temple, an Indian wigwam, or by the wild Arab of the great desert with his face turned towards Mecca.

MEMOIRS

PENN'S TREATY WITH THE INDIANS 1681
(ca. 1847)

Hicks was a better artist than historian; the date should be 1682. He copied Benjamin West's famous canvas, probably through the medium of Boydell's engraving. Formal artists of the period, such as West, learned their craft by copying the works of masters. Primitives like Hicks went a step further and frankly appropriated the work of others in whole, as here, or in details. The primitives' knowledge of formal art and design patterns came through engravings in an age without color reproductions. Hicks honored Penn, Quaker founder of Pennsylvania, for the extraordinary liberties he accorded his colony. The Liberty Bell itself was cast—long before American independence—to commemorate the fiftieth anniversary of Penn's Charter of Privileges of 1701.

Courtesy, Mr. and Mrs. Robert Carlen. Photograph from the Department of State.

WM. PENN'S *TREATY* with the INDIAN'S *1681*.

Peaceable Kingdom with Quakers

And I soon got into a state like the man in the fable, who got his neighbors faults and his own into a wallet, but in putting it on his shoulder he got his own faults behind and his neighbors before his eyes, where he could always see them. Thus I got to be a great talker, and a great fault finder, . . . Thus I went staggering along, still keeping my neighbors faults in the fore-end of the wallet, and my own behind my back, till I met with a female Friend in the ministry, at the house of a particular friend of mine, where I was talking in my usual style, until I noticed a peculiar solemnity and silence in the countenance of the woman that alarmed me, and seizing the wallet, she soon turned it end for end. At the sight of my own faults I fled from her with precipitancy. Her husband followed me for some distance, affectionately requesting me to stop. But I went home resolving to talk less and pray more. And now having a better view of my own faults, I lost sight of my neighbors, . . .

MEMOIRS

PEACEABLE KINGDOM WITH QUAKERS BEARING BANNERS (ca. 1832)

The Orthodox-Hicksite controversy has provoked anger on the faces of the carnivorous animals. Elias Hicks, Edward's cousin and storm center of the conflict, stands with handkerchief in hand in the forefront of a pyramidal group of Quakers. Streamers proclaiming "Peace on earth, good will to men" bind these Friends to Christ and the Apostles on the mountain top. But the curious lack of centrality in the composition connotes a basic disunity. The painting was inspired by the artist's Bucks County friend, Samuel Johnson, who wrote a poem suggesting the "Progress of Religious Liberty" as a theme.

GOOD-WILL to MEN

PEACEABLE KINGDOM

Grave of William Penn

4th *month, 7th and 8th* [1846]. To-day I think I have been edified and encouraged in reading two of dear William Penn's sermons, preached more than one hundred and fifty years ago. Oh! the unity and love I feel for that precious Friend. . . . One of the sermons was preached at a wedding when a Quaker wedding was a serious thing, a solemn religious institution. But now our excellent discipline is too much changed into a civil concern, and I fear is too much like the labor saving and money saving machinery of the day.

MEMOIRS

GRAVE OF WILLIAM PENN (1847)

A more literal mood is expressed in this tranquil landscape. Edward Hicks was violently anti-British, but this was one spot in England which he loved, although he had never seen it. Penn and his family were buried beneath the shade trees at Jordans Meeting House, Buckinghamshire. The scene was apparently borrowed from a Dutch painter, and Hicks added the great brindled bull and suckling lamb of his farm-scapes. He also gave the shepherd a plain Quaker hat! Inscribed on the original stretcher is, "Painted by E. Hicks in his 68th year. For his Friend, Ann Drake."

The Grave of Wm PENN at Jordans in England.

Peaceable Kingdom

4*th month, 20th* [1846]. Industriously engaged at my trade or business —working with my own hands to provide things honest in the sight of all men, ministering to my own necessities and them that are with me, which always produces peace of mind to an humble, honest Christian.

MEMOIRS

PEACEABLE KINGDOM (1844)

Commissioned by Joseph Watson, a prominent Friend of Middletown Township, Bucks County, this *Kingdom* presents many new creatures from verses 7 and 8 of Isaiah's prophecy; Richard Westall, Hicks's model, had used only those in verse 6. This painting marks a turning point in the development of the *Kingdoms*. Now strongly centered, the composition forms a superb triangle of leopard, ox, and lion. These are no longer mere animals, but archetypes reflecting human character. The grape branch has vanished—too orthodox an emblem in the recent Orthodox-Hicksite controversy. But, in the background, the child is attempting to yoke the young lion, the calf, and the fatling together—a task of reconciliation which will bear fruit later.

The Residence of David Twining 1787

David Twining was one of the most respectable, intelligent, and wealthy farmers in the county of Bucks, having been chosen one of the Provincial Assembly, though an exemplary member of the Society of Friends. His wife, Elizabeth, was just such a woman as is described in the last chapter of Proverbs. . . . It was this woman that it seems was providentially appointed to adopt me as a son, and to be to me a delegated shepherdess, under the great Shepherd and Bishop of souls. She had the simplicity and almost the innocence of a child. Being deprived of her parents in her childhood, and left poor, she received no scholastic education, only learning to read after she was grown up; yet she read the Scriptures with a sweetness, solemnity, and feeling I never heard equalled. How often have I stood, or sat by her, before I could read myself, and heard her read, particularly the 26th chapter of Matthew. . . . It was there that all the finer feelings of my nature were concentrated in love to my blessed Saviour.

MEMOIRS

THE RESIDENCE OF DAVID TWINING 1787 (1845–48)

Nostalgia and a yearning for inward peace lure the artist back to his childhood. Edward, aged seven, stands at the knee of his foster mother, Elizabeth, who reads from the Bible on her lap. Her husband, David Twining, stands nearby. Their daughter, Mary Twining Leedom, and her husband mount their horses, a pose borrowed from *Washington at the Delaware*. In the background is the Twining home, a typical Pennsylvania farmhouse of fieldstone, which is still standing today.

Noah's Ark

For if the Lord preserve us in our lives and conversation, in going in and out, we shall live in peace, in our families and neighbourhoods, and the God of grace will be with us. This will be our portion, if we are attentive to the light. And then, whatever trials and troubles we may meet with, whatever losses and crosses, although we be stripped of our nearest and dearest friends and earthly comforts—the Lord will be to us a friend, and his arm will be underneath to bear us up above the rolling, tempestuous billows.

CARPENTERS' HALL SERMON

NOAH'S ARK (1846)

Primitive imagery and maturing technique unite in this masterpiece. The toylike charm is there, seen through a lens of emotional and spiritual depth. Here is a summation of all Hicks's animals: to the beasts of *Kingdom* and farmscape are added those of jungle, pampas, and veldt, "two and two of all flesh, wherein is the breath of life." These are beasts and only beasts, except for the lion, whose eyes remind us that the Ark, too, was a source of salvation. Copied from a lithograph by Nathaniel Currier.

Pastoral Landscape

I quit the only business I understood, and for which I had a capacity, viz. painting, for the business of a farmer, which I did not understand, and for which I had no qualifications whatever. I verily thought then, and still think, *farming* more consistent with the Christian, and was willing to sacrifice all my fondness for painting. But it would not do, for notwithstanding I worked hard, I went behind hand daily. . . . But there is something of importance in the example of the primitive Christians and primitive Quakers, to mind their callings or business, and work with their own hands at such business as they are capable of, avoiding idleness and fanaticism. Had I my time to go over again I think I would take the advice given me by my old friend Abraham Chapman, a shrewd, sensible lawyer that lived with me about the time I was quitting painting; "Edward, thee has now the source of independence within thyself, in thy peculiar talent for painting. Keep to it, within the bounds of innocence and usefulness, and thee can always be comfortable."

MEMOIRS

PASTORAL LANDSCAPE (1845–49)

A growing sophistication of technique and the absence of the ideological content which was so much a part of Hicks's primitivism are evident here. There are echoes of the *Grave of William Penn* in the shepherd and his dog racing after their sheep, and of *The Residence of David Twining* in the bovine resting beneath the tree. This was painted for Charles Leedom, son of Jesse and Mary Twining Leedom, and brother of David Leedom, for whom Hicks executed *The Leedom Farm*.

Abby Aldrich Rockefeller Folk Art Collection.

The Leedom Farm

Where, then, can a man find so much comfort and enjoyment as in the bosom of his own family, where all is peace, all quietness,—and where the children are all walking in divine order, and coming up in the nurture and admonition of the Lord. It will lead to a greater enjoyment of the things of this world than any thing else. And we can avail ourselves of it in no other way, but by attending to the light, and walking in the light, as God is in the light; and when we do this, we shall have fellowship one with another. Then all this bitterness, bickering, finding fault with one another, and backbiting will be done away.

CARPENTERS' HALL SERMON

THE LEEDOM FARM (1849)

Inscribed "A May morning view of the farm and stock of David Leedom of Bucks County, Pennsylvania, with a representation of Himself, Wife, Father, Mother, Brothers, Sisters, and nephew. Painted by Edward Hicks in the 70th year of his age." Across the canvas flows a gentle progression of barnyard creatures: the lordly bull, cows ready for milking, the ewe and lamb of which the painter was so fond. Red roofs lend an accent to the muted colors of this orderly Quaker realm.

Peaceable Kingdom

Finally, my friends, farewell! May the melancholy be encouraged and the sanguine quieted; may the phlegmatic be tendered and the choleric humbled; may self be denied and the cross of Christ worn as a daily garment; may his peaceable kingdom for ever be established in the rational, immortal soul; then will be fulfilled the prophetic declaration of the infinitely wise Jehovah, through his evangelical prophet—"The wolf also shall dwell with the lamb, and the leopard shall lie down with the kid; the calf, and the young lion, and the fatling together, and a little child shall lead them; the cow and the bear shall feed, their young shall lie down together, and the lion shall eat straw like the ox. The sucking child shall play upon the hole of an asp, and the weaned child shall put its hand on the cockatrice's den. Nothing shall hurt or destroy in all my holy mountain, for the earth shall be full of the knowledge of the Lord, as the waters cover the sea."

MEMOIRS

PEACEABLE KINGDOM (ca. 1849)

This painting is almost identical to the artist's last *Kingdom*. Friendly beasts extend themselves in the mellow light. The leopard has grown magnificently serene. The old lion shares the straw of the vegetarian ox, as a token of humility. And the young lion fixes us with a last look, as he and the calf and the fatling together follow the little child into the Kingdom of the Spirit.

The Galerie St. Etienne, New York.

The wolf with the lambkin dwells in peace
  his grim carnivorous thirst for blood will cease;
The beauteous leopard with his restless eye,
  shall by the kid in perfect stillness lie;

The calf, the fatling and young lion wild,
  shall all be led by one sweet little child;
The cow and the bear shall quietly partake
  of the rich food the ear and corn stalk make;

While each their peaceful young with joy survey
  as side by side on the green grass they lay;
While the old lion thwarting nature's law
  shall eat beside the ox the barley straw.

The illustrious Penn this heavenly Kingdom felt
  Then with Columbia's native sons he dealt,
Without an oath a lasting treating made
  In Christian faith beneath the elm tree's shade.